better together*

*This book is best read together, grownup and kid.

 **akidsco.com**

a kids book about

a kids book about

THE TULSA RACE MASSACRE

by **Carlos Moreno**
Author of ***The Victory of Greenwood***

a
kids
book
about

Printed in the United States of America.

A Kids Book About books are available online: *akidsco.com*

To share your stories, ask questions, or inquire about bulk
purchases (schools, libraries, and nonprofits), please use
the following email address: *hello@akidsco.com*

ISBN: 978-1-953955-02-9

Designed by Rick DeLucco
Edited by Denise Morales Soto

Title treatment and interior display text
set in Martin by Vocal Type Foundry.

This book is dedicated to the elders of Greenwood, who welcomed me and told me their stories so that I could pass them along to others. I am forever grateful to have learned from them.

Intro

Between the 1890s and 1920s, a wave of massacres and attacks on Black communities swept the nation. The worst of these happened in the Greenwood neighborhood in Tulsa, Oklahoma, between May 31 and June 1, 1921.

This event remains the most destructive and deadly domestic terrorist attack in American history. 100 years later, television shows, documentaries, and other media have elevated the 1921 Tulsa Race Massacre to a national conversation, while cities everywhere are trying to find ways to end systemic racial violence. Newly discovered historical documents and eyewitness accounts are breaking myths about the Tulsa Race Massacre. Tulsa is still learning more about Greenwood's rebuilding post-1921—a story of community, resilience, and hope—which can help inspire us all to see our shared humanity.

This book is about
the Tulsa Race Massacre.

But before we can understand what that is, we need to learn about

GREENWOOD.

Greenwood is a neighborhood in Tulsa, Oklahoma, founded in 1905[1] by a group of Black people.*

*Before 1905, the land was owned by tribes of the Cherokee and Muscogee (Creek) nations.[2]

[1]Western Judicial District Indian Territory, deed of Greenwood, 30 December 1905, Tulsa, OK, Land Records Book N: 252, Tulsa County Court Clerk microfilm 11606.
[2]Angie Debo, *And Still the Waters Run: The Betrayal of the Five Civilized Tribes*, Second Edition (Princeton, NJ: Princeton University Press, 2020).

Over the course of 15 years, it grew into a thriving community of around 10,000 people and hundreds of businesses.

Many things made
Greenwood special.

It was an accepting, diverse
neighborhood full of...

HOPE.

Greenwood was also
a place of innovation.

It was the birthplace of the first Black daily national newspaper in the US, and the home of the most successful Black-owned hotel in the country.[3]

[3]Andrew J. Smitherman, "Andrew J. Smitherman: a Pioneer of the African American Press, 1909-1961.," The Free Library (Afro-Americans in New York Life and History, July 1, 2010); Steve Gerkin, "First Charged, Last Freed," *This Land Press*, March 20, 2014.

Black women, like **Loula Williams,**
owned many businesses.

She owned candy stores,
movie theaters, and offices
she rented to other
business owners.[4]

[4]Tim Madigan, *The Burning: Massacre, Destruction, and the Tulsa Race Riot of 1921* (New York, NY: St. Martin's Publishing Group, 2003).

This was a time when Black people could not purchase land in white neighborhoods.

But in Greenwood, they could own land and thrive.

Another thing that made Greenwood special was that it was located along the railroad tracks.

The railroad was very important back then.

Not only was it a means of transportation and connecting people all across the country, it was also an important resource for doing business.

(Think of it as the internet of the 1900s.)

Greenwood had clothing stores,
shoe and hat stores,
movie theaters, jazz clubs,
grocery stores, 2 schools,
a hospital, a skating rink,
and lots of ice cream
and candy shops.

GREENWOOD WAS SIMPLY AN AMAZING PLACE.

BUT...

There were white men who recognized the wealth and success of Greenwood and didn't want the Black people of Greenwood to have any.

They wanted it for themselves.

They also wanted to build their own train depot in Greenwood and make even more money for themselves.

So they decided to take control of the whole area.[5]

[5]Dreisen Heath, "The Case for Reparations in Tulsa, Oklahoma," *Human Rights Watch*, May 29, 2020.

All of this is what led to the event we know today as the Tulsa Race Massacre.*

*A massacre is the act of killing many people at once, who are usually helpless or unresisting, for no reason other than cruelty.

Now, you may have heard stories about what happened that day and why it happened, but it's a lot more complicated than you think.

When talking about the
Tulsa Race Massacre we often
hear the name, Dick Rowland.

Dick Rowland was a Black man
who was accused of hurting a white
woman named Sarah Page.

Dick Rowland was arrested on the morning of May 31, even though Sarah Page said the accusations against him were false.[6]

Later that night, a gunfight broke out in front of the courthouse jail where he was being held.

[6] Randy Krehbiel, *Tulsa, 1921: Reporting a Massacre* (Norman, OK: University of Oklahoma Press, 2021).

BUT THAT'S NOT THE ENTIRE STORY.

That's only 1 of the things that happened on that day, and it wasn't the cause of this massacre.

The Tulsa Race Massacre
happened on the morning of

JUNE 1, 1921.

The white men in power saw Dick Rowland's arrest as a chance to carry out their plan.[7]

[7]Jackson Undertaking Co. vs The City of Tulsa, Oklahoma, et al. Case No. 23371 (Tulsa Historical Society & Museum May 31, 1937); Walter F. White, "Desires of Pan-African Congress Presented In Resolutions," *The Dallas Express*, October 22, 1921.

Now, who were these white men in power?

Well, there were a few.

There was...

T.D. EVANS,
who was the mayor of Tulsa.[8]

JOHN GUSTAFSON,
who was the chief of police.[9]

HARRY SINCLAIR,
who was a wealthy man
in the oil business.[10]

AND TATE BRADY,
who was the local
leader of the KKK.*[11]

The KKK stands for Ku Klux Klan, which is a white supremacist terrorist hate group who primarily target and attack Black people.

[8]Randy Krehbiel, "Root of the Riot," *Tulsa World*, last modified May 21, 2020.
[9]The Archive of American Journalism, "Fraud and Corruption in Office Charged Against Chief," *Daily Ardmoreite*, June 26, 1921.
[10]Steve Gerkin, "The Trouble with Harry," This Land Press, March 28, 2012, Richard S. Warner, *Tulsa Race Riot A Report by the Oklahoma Commission to Study the Tulsa Race Riot of 1921* (Oklahoma City, OK: Oklahoma Historical Society, 2001).
[11]Lee Roy Chapman, "The Nightmare of Dreamland," *This Land Press*, April 18, 2012.

All of these men, leading up to the Tulsa Race Massacre, were putting together their plan to take Greenwood and move the Black community north, away from the railroad tracks.

ON THAT DAY....

More than 200 white people
began to loot and burn
Greenwood homes
and stores.

Planes dropped bombs to make the fires burn faster.

More than 1,200 homes were burned down.

And more than 300 people were killed.[12]

This can be a very painful thing to think about,

AND THAT'S OK.

[12]Report, Tulsa Race Riot Disaster Relief, American Red Cross, Report, Tulsa Race Riot Disaster Relief (Tulsa, OK: Tulsa Historical Society & Museum, 1994).; Madigan, *The Burning: Massacre, Destruction, and the Tulsa Race Riot of 1921*.

You might be wondering,
why did this happen?

Why would anyone do
something like this?

Remember what we said earlier?

THE WHITE MEN IN POWER WANTED MORE WEALTH.

To try to get it, they set up
an elaborate plan to steal it
from the Black people
of Greenwood.[13]

[13]Walter F. White, "I Investigate Lynchings," *American Mercury Magazine*, January 1, 1929, 81.

Nothing about what
happened on that day
was a coincidence.

They prepared 3 areas
for internment camps.*

Airplanes were prepared.

Bombs were made.

Guns and dynamite
were stockpiled.

And when they carried
out their plan...

*An internment camp is a prison made for innocent people.

many people died, many lost their homes and businesses, and those who survived were rounded up and marched to the internment camps.[14]

[14]Report, American Red Cross, Report, Tulsa Race Riot Disaster Relief (Tulsa, OK: Tulsa Historical Society & Museum, 1994); Madigan, *The Burning: Massacre, Destruction, and the Tulsa Race Riot of 1921*; Walter F. White, "The Eruption of Tulsa," *The Nation* (The Nation, August 23, 2001).

The story of the
Tulsa Race Massacre
is hard to tell and
hard to read.

But thankfully,

THAT'S NOT THE END OF THE STORY.

The people of Greenwood were resilient and didn't let this tragedy define them.

They started rebuilding immediately.

While some people left, most Greenwood residents refused to leave or sell their land.

In fact, the very next day, Loula Williams visited her lawyer.

Together, they made a plan to rebuild her numerous businesses, including her movie theater.[15]

[15]Ruth Sigler Avery Collection. Series 1: Tulsa Race Massacre of 1921. Oklahoma State University-Tulsa Library Archives.

On behalf of the people
of Greenwood, 2 Black lawyers—
B.C. Franklin and I.H. Spears—
sued the city, the mayor, the
police department, and the
powerful white men
and won their case![16]

[16] Joe Lockard vs. T.D. Evans, et al. Case No.15730 (Tulsa Historical Society & Museum August 25, 1921).

The American Red Cross helped rebuild.

They set up shelters and a clinic to help the people who were hurt or left homeless.[17]

[17]American Red Cross, Report, Tulsa Race Riot Disaster Relief (Tulsa, OK: Tulsa Historical Society & Museum, 1994).

And the members of
Vernon AME church donated
what money they could—
25 cents, 50 cents, 1 dollar—
to help rebuild their church.[18]

[18] *Book of Members and Donations*, 1921–1928 (Tulsa, OK: Historic Vernon AME Church, n.d.).

The white men in power lost, and eventually, Greenwood was restored.

A few years later, Greenwood was a thriving, vibrant neighborhood once again.[19]

[19] "Solomon Sir Jones Films, 1924–1928," Beinecke Rare Book & Manuscript Library (Yale Collection of Western Americana, January 25, 2021); Wendy Shay, "Black Wall Street on Film: A Story of Revival and Renewal," National Museum of American History (National Museum of American History, Behring Center, February 24, 2017).

Now...

what can we learn from
the people of Greenwood?

Pieces of this story
still exist today.

In cities across the country.

In small towns.

And maybe even in
your neighborhood.

There is still an
imbalance of power.

There is still hate.

Race divisions are
bigger than ever.

And there are still
systems that keep these
divisions in place.

But...

WE CAN

DO BETTER.

We can learn from history
and we can change things.

The Greenwood of today is still about neighbors helping neighbors, businesses supporting one another, and community—as much as it was in the days following the massacre.

So like the people who
fought to rebuild Greenwood,
keep the community alive,
and support one another...

YOU CAN DO THE SAME.

You have the power to make history and keep the tragedies of the past from repeating themselves.

Outro

Despite every attempt to steal their land, the people of Greenwood resisted. They began rebuilding their homes and businesses the day after they were attacked. In 1925, Reverend Solomon Sir Jones filmed Greenwood's thriving community, which you can see today online. People like Otis Clark, Olivia Hooker, Earl Bostic, Mary E. Jones Parrish, Ben Hill, Loula Williams, Amos T. Hall, E.L. and Jeanne Goodwin, and Emmit J. McHenry broke racial barriers and shaped American history.

Through their stories, I connected to Greenwood with my heart. I hope this book inspired you to learn about them, and maybe about the people in a neighborhood near you. It's amazing what we can learn from each other's stories.

Further Reading:

Black Fortunes: The Story of the First Six African Americans Who Escaped Slavery and Became Millionaires by Shomari Wills

My Life and An Era: The Autobiography of Buck Colbert Franklin by B.C. Franklin

The Nation Must Awake: My Witness to the Tulsa Race Massacre of 1921 (original title: *Events of the Tulsa Disaster*) by Mary E. Jones Parrish

They Came Searching: How Blacks Sought the Promised Land in Tulsa by Eddie Faye Gates

The Burning: Massacre, Destruction, and the Tulsa Race Riot of 1921 by Tim Madigan

IN HONOR OF THOSE LOST IN THE TULSA RACE MASSACRE

ED ADAMS, GREG ALEXANDER, EARNEST AUSTIN
F.M. BAKER, HARRY BARKER, HOWARD BARRENS,
JOHN BERRELL, TOM BRYANT, HOMER CLINE,
GEORGE WALTER DAGGS, CARRIE DIAMOND, RUBEN
EVERETT, JAMES GREESON, GEORGE HAWKINS,
ROBERT C. HAWKINSON, CLARENCE HILL, EDWARD
G. HOWARD, BILLY HUDSON, ANDREW C. JACKSON
ARTHUR JANES, GEORGE JEFFERY, ED LOCKARD
CHARLES D. LOTSPEICH, JOE MILLER, UNKNOWN
MORRISON, JAMES PARIS, S. H. PIERCE, SAM
REE, BROOKS ROBERTS, HARRY ROBERTS, M.M
SANDRIDGE, LEWIS SHELTON, T.J. SHERRILL
CLEO SHUMATE, UNKNOWN TALBOT, UNKNOWN
TALBOT, CUALEY WALKER, HENRY WALKER
G.E. WEAVER, JOHN WHEELER, J.H. WILSON
IRA JAMES WITHROW, SAMUEL J. WITHROW,